Job-Hunting
on the Internet

The Parachute Library

Job-Hunting on the Internet

Richard Nelson Bolles

Ten Speed Press
Berkeley, California

Ten Speed Press
P.O. Box 7123
Berkeley, California 94707

Distributed in Australia by E. J. Dwyer Pty. Ltd., in Canada by Publishers
Group West, in New Zealand by Tandem Press, in South Africa by Real
Books, in Singapore and Malaysia by Berkeley Books, and in the United
Kingdom and Europe by Airlift Books.

Cover design by Fifth Street Design
Interior design by Star Type, Berkeley

Library of Congress Cataloging-in-Publication Data
Bolles, Richard Nelson.
     Job hunting on the Internet / Richard Nelson Bolles.
        p.   cm.
     Includes bibliographical references and index.
     ISBN 0-89815-909-1
     1. Job hunting—United States—Computer network resources.
   2. Web sites—United States—Directories.   I. Title.
   HF5382.75.U6B65   1996
   025.06'65014—dc21

                                        96-37034
                                        CIP

First printing, 1997
Printed in the United States of America

1 2 3 4 5 6 7 8 9 10 — 01 00 99 98 97

Table of Contents

CONCLUSION

Appendix

Acknowledgments

I want to begin by expressing my great debt of gratitude to those who gave me help in understanding and navigating the Internet, during these past two years: my friend Guy Kawasaki, Margaret Riley, Mary Ellen Mort, Nick Donatiello, Martin Kimeldorf, Clara Horvath, Deborah Bryant, and Jamie Hammond. But most of all I want to express my gratitude for the immeasurable help I have received from my son, Gary Bolles, former editor-in-chief of *Network Computing* Magazine, and former editor-in-chief of *Inter@ctive Week* Magazine. He is one of the leaders in the field, and has been a fountainhead of knowledge and technical know-how for me.

Needless to say, none of the above are responsible for any of the opinions expressed in this book, or for any misstatement of facts which may be here, for which I alone am responsible.

Job-Hunting
on the
Internet

The Current Situation

If it has escaped your notice that there is a thing called the *Internet* (in general) and the *World Wide Web* (in particular), congratulations! You have *really* managed to get away from it all this past year or two, haven't you!

These two entities seem omnipresent in our society, right now. *Web addresses* appear at the bottom of loads of movie ads, not to mention at the bottom of ads for everything else that moves.

Many newspapers have a column or section that publishes new *Web addresses*, or URLs -- like:

http:www.washingtonpost.com/parachute

each week. Internet addicts, of course, collect new URLs as though they were baseball cards.

Local bookstores have whole sections devoted to the Web and the Internet. And, included among these are a goodly number of books devoted to job-hunting on the Internet *(See "Further Reading" on page 107).*

From all of this, you might be forgiven for thinking that everyone is on the Internet except you, poor modemless person that you are or have been. Well, take heart. You are not as *out of it* as you think.

Individual usage is difficult to assess; household usage is easier. In terms of households, this is the current situation -- despite all the *hype* to the contrary:

At Home

37% of American households have a computer at home	**63% do not**
24% of American households have a modem, and could be online	**76% do not**
16% of American households are actually online, one way or another	**84% are not**
0.07% -- or less than one tenth of one percent -- of American households do job-hunting online	**99.93% do not**

At Work or School

As best the experts can guesstimate, this is the current situation there:

Over 60% of Internet activity takes place at work, and is, of course, work-related in the majority. 25% of all Americans 16 years of age or older have access to the Internet at work or school	**75% do not**
21.5% of all Americans 16 years of age or older actually access the Internet, at least on occasion, at home or work or school	**78.5% never do**
8% of the population actually access the Internet *regularly*	**92% do not**

(These statistics are the latest available as of 1/27/97, and are from a number of sources, above all Nick Donatiello, President of Odyssey, a noted market research firm. See: www.the site.com/1196w5/work/work293_112696.html)

Of course, if you are already online yourself, the above statistics will seem dead wrong to you, because virtually every friend you have will also be online.

It reminds one of the old joke about Sigmund Freud, which was, that he thought the whole world was filled with nothing but neurotics or psychotics, because those were the only people he ever saw. It is hard to remember that your *sample* of the general population -- the people you attract, and hob-nob with -- is greatly skewed by your interests and pursuits. *"Birds of a feather flock together . . . "*

Your impressions aside, the survey evidence is that *currently* most American households (about 84% of the U.S., anyway) are not on the Internet *with any regularity*, if at all -- in spite of the hype and the omnipresence of the Internet in the news. Indeed, disenchantment sets in even among those who do use the Internet: the average user is currently online only 12 hours a month, compared to the figure of 16 hours a month a year ago. And, 40% of all users spend less than two hours a week online.

This is bound to change, of course; only 4% of U.S. households were on the Internet a couple of years ago; last year, 8%; this year, 16%. Moreover, communication companies -- such as cable companies, phone companies, computer manufacturers, television manufacturers, and Internet Service Providers -- are forming new partnerships weekly if not daily, and working day and night, toward the goal (someday) of the Internet being as easy to use as turning on a TV, or picking up a telephone -- using a hardware device costing less than $350, that employs your TV as its screen, and your cable or phone line as its Internet connection. WebTV has already begun, in this direction.

For those 84% of American households that are not on the Internet yet, but may be idly thinking about it --and most particularly for those job-hunters, career-changers, and career-counselors, who are currently *Net-less* -- and puzzled, curious, and toying with the idea, I offer a Beginner's Primer of what the Internet -- and *the Web* -- are all about, in the Appendix at the end of this book, beginning on page 87.

Many of my readers, however, will already be familiar with this stuff, and will want to proceed directly to the issue of, how to use the Internet for job-hunting. So, it is to that subject that I now turn.

An Outline of This Guide

There are five ways in which the Internet can be helpful to job-hunters or career-changers. They are:

#1. As a place for you to search for **vacancies**, listed by employers (often called **job listings**).

#2. As a place to post your **resume**.

#3. As a place to get some job-hunting help or **career counseling**.

#4. As a place to make **contacts** with people, who can help you find information, or help you get in for an interview, at a particular place.

#5. As a place to find **information** or do **research** on fields, occupations, companies, cities, etc.

I have used these five headings (**Job Listings, Resumes, Career Counseling, Contacts,** and **Research**) as the outline for this Guide -- plus a sixth, **Gateway Sites,** that I will explain shortly. But first, let me explain my rating system.

Parachute Picks

MY PERSONAL RATING SYSTEM

There are alleged to be 11,000 sites on the Internet that deal with jobs, careers, or job-hunting. The number grows weekly.

I have listed the most useful sites *that I know of* (but, in spite of my spending as many as 7 hours a day on the Internet, I'm just sure there are a lot of good sites that I know nothing about).

All sites listed in this book are better than average, in my opinion.

Of these, I've selected a few that I think are especially good sites *within their category* and given them a Parachute symbol.

= I think, for job-hunting purposes, this is one of the best sites on the Net, *in its category (the categories are: Gateway Sites, Job-Posting Sites, Resume Sites, Career Counseling Sites, Contacts Sites, and Research Sites)*

And now, let us begin with the large indexes of job-hunting sites on the Net, that I have called "Gateway Sites."

Incidentally, this booklet's URLs and evaluations, are on the Web, at:

http://www.
washingtonpost.com/parachute

and, for those of you who think I omitted an important site, that you have discovered and found helpful in your job-hunt, you can send your suggestion to an e-mail address, there:

parachute@washpost.com

*As you enter these addresses into your favorite
search engine on the Web, please remember that
all URLs in this booklet are to be typed,
by you, without any spaces whatsoever,
from start to finish,
even if they spill over on to more than
one line in the text here.*

Web Addresses
for Job-Hunters and
Career-Changers

Gateway Sites

If you were to start from scratch, find your favorite Internet search engine, and ask it to do a search on the keywords: "careers," "jobs," "employment," "resumes," "job listings," "career counseling," and the like, you would turn up a sizeable list.

But you don't need to start from scratch. *Fortunately,* a lot of people have already done this search, for you.

Their results are posted at the following *large, gateway* job-sites:

The Riley Guide

http://www.jobtrak.com/jobguide/

This is the best, by far. If I could only go to one *gateway* job-site on the Web, this would be it.

But there are others, which have done a fine job of putting together summary lists of what's available. We'll start with:

Job Hunt: A Meta-List of Online Job-Services

http://rescomp.stanford.edu/jobs/

You *may* need to increase the memory assigned to your Web browser, first, before mouse-clicking on this site, as this is a *huge* file. Incidentally, this site has *its own* rating system for the career sites it lists.

Emory Colossal List of Career Links

http://www.emory.edu/CAREER/Links.html

This is sponsored by Emory University's career center ("Career Paradise") in Atlanta, Georgia. This site also has its own rating system, called the CareerMeister Rating, on two scales: functionality, and artistic impression. The listings are amusingly described.

Magellan

http://www.mckinley.com/

This search engine's "Career and Employment" section rates its sites in a really helpful way. I like it.

Job Search and Employment Opportunities: Best Bets from the Net

```
http://www.lib.umich.edu/chdocs/
employment/
```

I don't agree with some of its selections (as "Best"), but it is very comprehensive.

Career Resource Center

```
http://www.careers.org/index.html
```

It lists over 11,000 links to jobs, employers, business, education, and career service professionals on the Web, plus 6,000 other career resources (including Australia and New Zealand, Japan, Germany, and United Kingdom as well).

InfoSeek Guide -- Jobs & Careers

```
http://guide-p.infoseek.com/
```

This search engine's "Jobs & Careers" section lists "similar pages" for each item. Great idea.

Yahoo! Employment

```
http://www.yahoo.com/Business_and_
Economy/Employment/
```

These search engines change their navigation about every three minutes. If this doesn't take you to where you want to go, go to their home page, and select.

Point's Top 5% -- Careers & Jobs

```
http://point.lycos.com/reviews/
database/buca.html
```

This is one of those sites that tries to choose "the best" in each category. Their criteria for choosing the top 5 percent related to "Careers and Jobs" depend on: content, presentation, and experience. You, of course, want the top 5 percent to be based on "effectiveness in finding a job." Keep this difference in mind as you explore this list.

And that concludes my listing of the large *gateway* sites for job-hunting on the Internet. Now, visit the one or ones you are curious about; when you are done, you can then choose any of the five sections that I have divided this guide into. As I said earlier, there are five ways in which the Internet can be helpful to job hunters or career changers. They are:

#1. As a place for you to search for **vacancies**, listed by employers (often called **job listings**).

#2. As a place to post your **resume**.

#3. As a place to get some job-hunting help or career **counseling**.

#4. As a place to make **contacts** with people, who can help you find information, or help you get in for an interview, at a particular place.

#5. As a place to find **information** or do **research** on fields, occupations, companies, cities, etc.

Let us look at each of these, in turn.

1.

Job Listings

Job Listings on the Internet

We come here to the sites that make many job-hunters salivate: the promise of access to millions of *vacancies, help-wanted ads,* or *job listings,*' listed on the Internet by employers. Indeed, one Web site kept track of its visitors and found that the largest number of those visitors -- 33% -- went to the job listings, as compared with 26% to the next most popular area there -- salary surveys -- and just 13% to the place where they could put their resume online.

How Effective?

My personal estimate of the effectiveness of Job Posting Sites on the Internet: **one percent**, if the job you're looking for is not computer-related; **40 percent** if it is. That is, out of every one hundred computer people who search job listings on the Internet, 40 of them will find a job as a result. I think 60 will not. And out of every 100 non-computer people who search job listings on the Internet, one of them will find a job as a result. I think 99 will not.

Job listings! What a lovely sound! *A new place to meet employers.* Thousands of job opportunities, listed on the Internet! Ah, yes. How true! But just keep in mind two teensy tiny little problems as you explore these job listings.

The first is this: people's naive vision of the Internet is that it offers one central, unified place, where you can find a list of all available jobs in your own geographical region, if not in the whole country. Unfortunately, the reality is that we currently have 11,000 sites on the Internet dealing with jobs or careers. So, if you want to find out what jobs are posted on the Internet, you have to go to hundreds if not thousands of different sites to find that out. Yuk!

What you will not believe, until it happens to you, is that it is possible to hunt through all these listings on the Internet, and *still* not find one job that interests you -- unless of course, you're in the computer field, in which case the Internet is essentially like striking it rich. How can this be? How can you strike out so dramatically? Well, that brings us to our second problem: the infamous *hidden job market.*

What that phrase means is that employers, generally speaking, prefer every other method of filling vacancies that there is, before they will resort to want-ads or job listings. For many if not most of them, want-ads or job listings are their *court of last resort*, used only after all other methods have failed. You can see this in the following diagram, starting at the bottom.

6 "I will place an ad to find some-one."

The way a typical job-hunter likes to hunt for a job (starts here)

Newspaper Ads

Resumes

5 "I will look at some resumes which come in, unsolicited."

Employment Agency for Lower Level Jobs

4 "I want to hire someone for a lower level job, from a stack of potential candidates that some agency has screened for me."

This is called 'a private employ-ment agency,' or - - if it is within the company - - 'the human resources department,' formerly the 'personnel department.' Incidentally, only 15% of all organizations have such an internal department.

Search Firm for Higher Level Jobs

3 "I want to hire someone for a higher level job, from among outstanding people who are presently working for another organization; and I will pay a recruiter to find this outstanding candidate for me."

The agency, thus hired by an employer, is called 'a search firm' or 'headhunter'; only employers can hire such agencies.

A Job-Hunter Who Offers Proof

2 "I want to hire someone who walks in the door and can show me samples of their previous work."

"I want to hire someone whose work a trusted friend of mine has seen and recommends."

That friend may be: mate, best friend, colleague in the same field, or colleague in a different field.

From Within

Employer's Thoughts:

1 "I want to hire someone whose work I have seen." (Promotion from within of a full-time employee, or promotion from within of a part-time employee; hiring a former consultant for a regular position (formerly on a limited contract); hiring a temp for a regular position; hiring a volunteer for a regular position.)

The way a typical employer prefers to fill vacancies (starts here)

Our Neanderthal Job-Hunting System

(We job-hunters, of course, prefer to start at the top of this diagram, and work down. That is why our job-hunting system in this country is so *Neanderthal*. We prefer to job-hunt in exactly the reverse order that employers do.)

But, back to the diagram, if employers can fill their job vacancies without resorting to want-ads or job listings, they will; in 80% of all cases, they succeed. Hence the familiar statistic, for *decades*: "80% of all jobs are never advertised." Never advertised on the Internet, nor anywhere else.

What all this means for you is this: by all means browse these job-listings. You may find just the opportunity you are looking for. But don't get discouraged if you don't. Only 20% of all available jobs in this country ever get advertised, by employers. The rest wait for you to find other ways of finding them.

Just post these words above your computer, and keep them ever in mind if you've spent hours surfing through page after page of job listings, and have found *nothing* that interests you:

**"There are tons of jobs out there,
that the Web knows nothing about!"**

Parachute Picks:
Vacancies or Job Listing Sites (Multiple)

To begin with, there are some sites that have put a number of job posting *search-engines* all on one page. We start with:

JobBank USA MetaSEARCH

http://www.jobbankusa.com/

It will give you 20 or more employment search engines, for vacancies, all on one page. An outstanding site!

SEARCH.COM

http://www.search.com/

This site will give you 17 or more employment search engines that have job listings, all on one page. Another very good site, in this category.

Internet Job Surfer

http://www.rpi.edu/dept/cdc/jobsurfer/

This is a site maintained by Rensselaer Polytechnic Institute. It has an impressively lengthy list of commercial organizations that provide job databases or resume listings (or other services). The organizations are indexed alphabetically. Many other countries are included. And the list was updated as of the very date I visited the site.

Connect

http://www.cabrillo.cc.ca.us/connect/
docs/Jobs.html

That stands for: **C**alifornia **O**ccupational **N**ews **Net**-work **E**mploying **C**omputerized **T**elecommunications. It has a fine listing of job boards and other places to find job listings, including (of course) California-oriented sites. I like this site, and found it helpful.

Infoseek Guide -- Company Job Offerings

http://guide-p.infoseek.com

It lists over 1,000 companies and gives you the ability to search all 1,000 sites at once, with a keyword of your own choosing -- though somewhat limited outside technology/business sites. "Teacher" turned up only 7 sites, "writer" turned up 156, nationwide.

100hot

http://www.100hot.com/

It will give you a mixture of company sites and job listing sites, including international sites.

Excite -- Job Directories Reviews

http://www.excite.com/

It rates the various sites thus listed, in an interesting way.

Point Top 5%

http://www.pointcom.com/

It will give you a number of sites, *some* of which deal with job listings.

Lycos/A2Z Job Classifieds
`http://a2z.lycos.com/`

A limited listing, in my opinion.

ZD Net Jobs Database
`http://www.zdnet.com/zdi/jobs/jobs.html`

This site is tied to the Monster Board (see below) and is sometimes very difficult to get into. If you have trouble, try later at night.

Parachute Picks:
Vacancies or Job Listing Sites (Individual)

Multiple listings aside, you will want to familiarize yourself with some of the better known individual sites, *which get listed again and again in various career indices.* You will already have come across many of these, if you used any of the multiple-site pages listed previously. As you view the sites below, keep in mind that *many* of them offer more than just *job listings.*

America's Job Bank

http://www.ajb.dni.us/

This site is maintained by the Dept. of Labor, U.S. Employment Service. It links 1,800 state Employment Service offices in the U.S., and typically lists approximately 250,000 jobs. A wonderful site, if job listings are what you are looking for -- allowing you to sort available jobs by a first, second, third, and last priority (e.g., state, city, title, salary, and/or new job).

Career Path

http://www.careerpath.com/

It claims (legitimately, I think) to be "the most visited job-related site on the Internet," with nearly 3 million *searches* per month. It lists *some or all of* the current week's and previous Sunday's *help wanted* ads from at least 22 major newspapers in the U.S. Consequently, on a typical day, you can search over 130,000 help wanted ads, and they add 250,000 new ads per month. I think this is a very useful site, *if* classified ads are what you are looking for.

CareerPost

http://jobs.washingtonpost.com

This site has job listings taken from the last two Sunday editions of *The Washington Post.*

Career Magazine

```
http://www.careermag.com/cgi-bin/
searchbanner.cgi
```

Now, I think this is a very interesting site. Every day it downloads, and indexes, all the job listings from the major Internet *jobs newsgroups*, and then offers keyword sifting through those listings, according to your skills, title, and preferred location. It also offers more information about employers than most online resources. Be forewarned, however, you can still strike out.

JobTrak

```
http://www.jobtrak.com/
```

This site lists over 2,100 new job listings each day -- for college students, graduates, and alumni. In fact, you must list the campus you are on, and get a password, before you can access the job listings. Since I'm not on a campus, and have forgotten every password anyone ever gave to me, naturally I can't evaluate the job listings at this site. *"I'm on the outside, looking in . . ."*

JobNet

```
http://www.westga.edu/~coop/jobs.html
```

This is a collection of resources from the Web, Usenet News, Gopher, and Listserve. I happen to like it, because it has jobs from the parts of the job-market so often ignored at other job listing sites (e.g., "outdoor careers," "training," and the like).

The World Wide Web Employment Office

```
http://www.harbornet.com/biz/office/
annex.html
```

This is a very interesting site, as it lists job posting sites by field or occupation, and this means *a wide spectrum* of fields, unlike some other sites I could name. This site has links not only to the U.S. but to other countries as well.

JobWeb/Catapult Employment Centers

```
http://www.jobweb.org/catapult/
jobsall.htm
```

Part of JobWeb, this site is maintained by the National Association of Colleges and Employers. Inside or outside of academia, it has a nice list of job search resources, including "Other Directories of Employment Resources," listed by geographical region.

LDOL CareerNet Want Ads

```
http://www.ldol.state.la.us:80/
career1/ldolcp.htm
```

This CareerNET Resource and Development Center, sponsored by the Louisiana Department of Labor, is one of my favorite sites. Here you will find an impressive list of job listings (heavily weighted toward Louisiana, naturally), but check out "Jobs by Field."

Parachute Picks:
Vacancies or Job Listing Sites (Famous)

Now *some* of the sites we just looked at are well-known; but there are others that are even more famous. The problem with *these* that I am about to share with you is that, so far as job listings are concerned, many if not most of them have a big Achilles heel: namely, lots of listings -- but across a relatively narrow spectrum of the 12,000+ occupations that are out there. Mostly just jobs in technology, business, and academia. You will look in vain for very many listings for teachers, artists, crafts-people, etc., etc. Internet *experts* like to say, "Yes, I know, I know; but the situation is changing." Indeed it is, but having roamed these sites for two years now, I'd have to say change toward listing more of the 12,000+ occupations that are "out there" is occurring at a speed that makes a glacier look like a greyhound.

Now, I'm going out of my way to accidentally offend a good many people, because of my concern about *you*. I don't want you to let these sites throw you into a de-pression. And believe me, they can -- if you *think* they work for everyone else except *you*.

Take my word for it, some of these sites have a won-derful interface, but often you will feel like Dorothy and her friends when they were first ushered into the chambers of the Wizard of Oz: wonderful stuff up front, but take care to look behind all that smoke and mir-rors. Often you can't. You can't tell what they have be-hind the curtain. Just remember this: no matter how many listings they claim to have, do not take it personally if you don't find *anything* in the area you're looking for. The problem is not with you; the problem is with the Internet, and the limited spectrum of the job-market that it (thus far) covers.

Having said that about these sites' job listings, let me add that these sites do many other things besides job listings (and often do them very well). Okay, here goes.

CareerMosaic

```
http://www.careermosaic.com/cm/
usenet.html
```

This is an immensely famous job site, but as far as job listings are concerned, I struck out again and again when I looked (in various geographical regions) for anything but technical or computer jobs. Don't get discouraged if there is nothing here in your field.

The Online Career Center

```
http://www.occ.com/occ/
```

This site, sponsored by a non-profit association of leading corporations, is another immensely famous job site, and (like Career Path, earlier, and The Monster Board below) also claims to be "the Internet's first and most frequently accessed career center." It is heavily weighted toward technical and computer-related jobs, and when you go to "Search by Industry," they give you home pages of companies rather than individual job listings. It does have a good listing of Career Fairs and

Events. And, of course, if you're looking for a computer-related or technical job, you may find this site very helpful.

The Monster Board Career Search

`http://www.monster.com:80/`

This also claims to be "the premier career site on the World Wide Web," with over 750,000 visitors per month. The site claims over 50,000 listings, with 1,500 new ones being added each week; it also features a career center, and resume listings as well. It still seems to me to suffer from the same problems as so many other sites: lots of listings, but in a relatively narrow portion of the total job market. Don't get discouraged if there is nothing here that interests you.

Career Resource Center -- Jobs

`http://www.careers.org/gen/all_gems.htm`

This site lists over 11,000 links to jobs, employers, business, education and career service professionals on the Web, plus 6,000 other helpful career resources (which includes Australia and New Zealand, Japan, Germany, and the United Kingdom as well). Unfortunately, job-posting-wise, it is more of a sampler than anything else. Of course, its samples may be what you're looking for. Still, don't get discouraged if there is nothing here that interests you.

CareerWeb -- Jobs

`http://www.cweb.com/homepage.html`

This is another "often-cited" site, but it has the same problem as so many other sites: not enough listings. For example, when I tried it, it only listed 33 accountant/banking/financial services jobs in the entire country. Don't get discouraged if there is nothing here that interests you.

E-Span Job Search

http://www.espan.com/js/js.html

They bill themselves as "Your Online Employment Connection." It's another famous site, but -- again -- seems to me to be heavily oriented toward technology/computer-related jobs. But if that's your cup of tea, go to it!

The Black Collegian JASS

http://www.black-collegian.com/jobsg.html

JASS means "Job Assistance Selection Service." This site, unfortunately, lists companies more than "Job Opportunities," and even this is more of a sampler than anything else. You are left to figure out whether or not the company needs anyone.

Parachute Picks: Vacancies or Job Listing Sites (Particular Kinds of Jobs)

The Law Employment Center

http://www.lawjobs.com

If you are a lawyer looking for work, this is emphatically the site to visit. It's sponsored by the *Law Journal*, and has an alive feeling that some of the other job listing sites lack.

Academe This Week -- Job Openings

http://chronicle.merit.edu/.
ads/.links.html

This site gives you the job listings in the current issue of the *Chronicle of Higher Education.* If it's faculty or research positions or other college or university jobs that you are looking for, this is the site to visit. (It also has some listings that are outside academe.)

Galaxy -- Employment -- Academic

http://galaxy.einet.net./GJ/
employment.html

This is another good source of job listings in academia.

Government jobs are to be found at a number of sites, including the following four:

The Federal Jobs Digest

`http://www.jobsfed.com/fedjob4.html`

They list from 2,000 to 4,000 active vacancies on a typical day. The site is absolutely up to the minute, and this is clearly *the place* to visit, if you're looking for a job with the federal government. Has helpful salary charts for various grade levels. Only one minor caveat: they do need secretaries ("Secreterial" *[sic]* was misspelled twice on the main menu, on the three times I visited this site).

FedWorld Federal Jobs Search

`http://www.fedworld.gov/jobs/`
`jobsearch.html`

This is an official U.S. government site, and has very similar listings to those found in *Federal Jobs Digest*, above, except that you must tap on *each* listing here, in order to find out where the job is and other details. I prefer the *Federal Jobs Digest* interface to this.

OPM's USAjobs

`http://www.usajobs.opm.gov/`

This is another of the U.S. Government's official sites for jobs and employment information. On my first visit to this Web site I was dismayed to note it had been a month since it was last updated -- according to their own admission. On my most recent visit, while it was now up to date, I was dismayed to discover it had a slim selection in a number of job categories. Again, I prefer the *Federal Jobs Digest.*

Federal Jobs Central

`http://www.fedjobs.com/`

You have to be a subscriber to access the job listings on this site. (Hourly online subscription begins at $45 for one hour.) They also publish *Federal Career Opportunities,* a bi-weekly printed listing of federal jobs that is mailed to you (at $39 for six issues) -- plus other tools (at a price) for the federal jobs hunter.

Cool Works

`http://www.coolworks.com/showme/`

Leisure jobs in national parks, resorts, cruise ships, camps, plus volunteering, are to be found here.

Summer Jobs World-Wide

`http://www.summerjobs.com/do/where`

The site to come to if you're looking for a summer job.

Peterson's Summer Programs for Kids/Teens

`http://www.petersons.com/summerop/`
`ssector.html`

The site to come to if you're looking for a summer program and you're a kid.

JobTrak Job Fair Calendar

http://www.jobtrak.com/cfc/show.html

This site is for those who want to go face to face with employers.

Monster Board Career Fair Info

http://199.94.216.77/careerfair.html

Likewise, I'm sure.

JobSmart -- Upcoming Career Fairs

http://jobsmart.org/resource/fairs/
jobfairs.htm

Still another career fair/job fair site.

Parachute Picks: Vacancies or Job Listing Sites (Elsewhere on the Net)

There are many other Web sites featuring *Job Listings/ Ads/Openings/Vacancies/Jobs Available.* Just type the word "jobs" into your favorite search engine.

In addition to the Web, there are Usenet Newsgroups on the Internet that have job listings/want ads. Lists of them can be found at the following three sites:

Yahoo! Jobs on Newsgroups

```
http://www.yahoo.com/Business_and_
Economy/Employment/Jobs/Usenet
```

Jobs Offered Newsgroups

```
http://darkwing.uoregon.edu/~liwang/
newsjob.html
```

CareerMag Search Job Listings -- Newsgroups

```
http://www.careermag.com/careermag/
news/searchform.html
```

Then there are bulletin board services (called BBSs), which used to be primarily, if not exclusively, *outside* the Web. Now, many of them can be accessed directly through the Web; a wonderful list of these has been compiled by a man named Richard Mark, on a very pretty site, which can be found at:

Richard Mark's SBI

```
http://dkeep.com/sbi.htm
```

Another complete list of BBSs both within and outside the Web, can be found at *Harry's Job Search BBS & Internet Hot List* (compiled by a remarkable man, the pioneering Harold Lemon):

Harry's Job Search BBS & Internet Hot List
`http://rescomp.stanford.edu/jobs/`
`jobs-bbs.html`

Finally, if you search every job listing there is, on all the above sites (shouldn't take more than 4 weeks), and you discover nothing, zip, nada, that interests you, and you're *truly* desperate, there is a list of Employment Agencies to be found at:

HandiLinks To Employment Agencies
`http://www.ahandyguide.com/cat1/e/`
`e126.htm`

But of course, in many cases, your local Yellow Pages might serve you just as well, or better.

(If you try all these job-listing sites, and still can't find a job, see page 79 ff.)

2.

Your Resume

Resume Sites on the Internet

Many job-hunters think this should be the very best use of the Internet for a job-hunter: being able to post your resume. Oh, my, oh my! Let's recall some simple truths, here: *a resume is a resume is a resume.* As readers of *What Color Is Your Parachute?* know, it usually is not a very effective job-hunting tool; normally, for every 1,470 resumes floating around out there in the world of work, only one job-offer is tendered and accepted.

And, I'm sorry to report, it doesn't get much better just because it's online. While it is obvious that some job-hunters' resumes do get seen by employers on the Internet, and do lead to a job, it is also obvious that in a depressingly-large number of cases, *nothing* happens. Zero. Zip. Nada.

What's the problem here? Why doesn't your resume get more results, *online?* Well, for a resume to work online, some employer:

- has got to be *desperate* to find someone like you,

- has got to be at the point, in their search for someone like you, that they are reduced to reading resumes,

- has got to then go online,

- has got to accidentally stumble across the site where you posted your resume, and then

- has got to take the time and trouble to read it, and then

- has got to take the time and trouble to print it out, in all its blah ASCII sameness.

Not only is this a big *pain in the neck* to employers, but there are *at least* 10 million U.S. employers (not to mention other countries) who don't even *think* of the Internet when it's time to hire. Not even *think* of the Internet?? Yes, believe it or not, the CEOs of some very *large* corporations, still haven't got a computer anywhere in sight in their office or in their secretary's office. Just an old faithful *IBM Selectric.* Down through the twentieth century, it has always been true: *job-hunters* flock to a new technology or job-hunting aid, but a comparatively much smaller proportion of *employers* do.

So, in many if not most cases, your beautiful resume is just sitting there on the Internet. And sitting there. And sitting there. And sitting there.

How Effective?

My personal estimate of the effectiveness of Resume sites on the Internet: **less than one half of one percent**, if the job you're seeking is not computer-related; **20 percent** effectiveness, if it is. That is: out of every 100 computer people who post their resume on the Internet, 20 of them will find a job as a result. I think 80 will not. And out of every 100 non-computer people who post their resume on the Internet, less than 1 of them will find a job as a result. 99 of them will not.

But, you're going to put your resume on the Internet, at either a Web or newsgroup site, anyway, aren't you? Sure, you are! It may not get you a job, but your friends will be impressed, when you tell them what you've done! *You?! On the Internet?! Wow!*

There are a number of guides online which tell you exactly *how* to do this, and exactly *where* to do this. They'll tell you the rules about scanning, and the rules about keywords, and so forth. These guides are listed below in the Parachute Picks of resume sites.

Just one caveat: do remember that posting your resume online is the equivalent of nailing your resume to a tree in the town square -- where every employer, solid citizen, salesperson, con-artist, pervert, and drunk can see it, and copy down whatever he (or she) wants from it, for follow-up. *Think about it!*

Gary Morris -- of the Union College Career Development Center Web site (http://apollo.union.edu/CDC/CDC.html) -- suggests that if you are posting your portfolio or resume to a public area (such as a Web site) or an online resume database, security should always be a consideration. Gary advises his students to "never include personal or contact information in the body of your resume for safety and security purposes."

I would say that you may want to give your phone number *('cause this is most employers' favorite way of contacting job-hunters)*, plus your e-mail address, but **not** your street address, nor business address, nor names of past employers or references *online.* You can always mail this information to an interested employer or recruiter *after* they have contacted you by phone or e-mail.

One final word about resumes *online:* since your resume is going to look *very bland* in plain old ASCII, stripped of all its lovely formatting and the "nice look" of the original, Martin Kimeldorf suggests that one sentence you may want to add at the end of your posted resume, is: "An attractive and fully formatted hard copy version of this document is available upon request."

Parachute Picks:
Sites to Help You Write a Resume

JobSmart
http://jobsmart.org/tools/resume/
index.htm

This site features the best overall summary about resumes on the Internet, that I have seen, written by Clara Horvath and Yana Parker. If I were interested in putting my resume on the Internet, and if I could visit only one resume site for guidance and help, this would surely be it. Yana is the author of the popular *Damn Good Resume Guide* series, while Clara teaches classes in this subject. They have a sample list of places on the Internet to post your resume, free and for-fee.

Joyce Lain Kennedy
http://www.wiley.co.uk/Promotions/
Kennedy/ActualMaterial.html

If you want to know how to write an electronic resume, Joyce Lain Kennedy is the most popular syndicated careers columnist in America, and the author of several books on electronic job-hunting. She has become an expert on Internet job-hunting. Unfortunately, this site only gives us a sample of her insights. It does tell us, however, that she emphasizes the importance of keywords in electronic resumes.

Career Center Job Search Gopher

```
gopher://merlin.hood.edu:9999/11gopher_
root:%5bcareer_center.job_search%5d
```

Speaking of which, an excellent long list of specific keywords for various professions can be found at this *gopher* site (assuming your Internet Service Provider gives you access to *gopherspace*).

Resumix ResumeBuilder

```
http://www.resumix.com/resume/
resume-form.html
```

If you want to actually build your resume online, there's a site that will lead you step-by-step through the compiling of a "plain vanilla" resume, and then format it for you, and submit it. The site is maintained by Resumix, Inc.

Intellimatch -- "Watson"

```
http://riga.intellimatch.com/
```

Well, to begin with, this is another one of those sites that *boasts* ("Internet's #1 Service for Matching Job Seekers & Employers"). They call their resume system "Watson" or the "Power Resume." Like Resumix, above, this system will lead you step-by-step (it takes an hour) through the putting together of your resume -- and then formats it in the HTML language that a Website reads so well. But, be aware that the list of skills that they offer you, to use in your resume, is actually a list of *knowledges* -- akin to the "keywords" that some of the sites above talk about -- and this is not exactly the same thing as "skills." (See *The 1997 What Color Is Your Parachute?*)

This site's unique feature: they say they will then match your resume to their employer database, to see if there is an intelligent match (hence "IntelliMatch"). Sounds great, and many reviewers have warmly saluted this *idea.* The idea *is* great. The problem is in the execution of it. As of the time I talked with them (10/9/96), they reported 50,000 resumes in their database, but only 100 employers. That's because, while they don't charge you, the job-hunter, they do charge each employer (the basic package costs an employer $5,000).

Parachute Picks:
Sites Where You Can Post Your Resume

When you've got your resume all done, one way or another, and want to post it on the Internet, there are good lists of resume posting sites at the following locations:

The World Wide Web Employment Office

http://www.harbornet.com/biz/office/
annex.html

This is an excellent site, as it lists resume sites by field or occupation, covering a wide spectrum of fields. Outstanding! It is also a resume site itself (fee-based) -- you can link your resume (posted elsewhere) to their site for $10/yr, or put it on their site (if it is not posted anywhere yet) for $40/yr. As I mentioned elsewhere in this book, this site is unusual in another way: it has links not only to the U.S. but to other countries as well.

Tripod -- Where to Send Your Resume

http://www.tripod.com/work/resume/
linklist.html

When last I visited, it only listed 22 resume sites; *but*, where it is different from other lists, is that it evaluates each site, *very* realistically. Hence, naturally I like it -- a lot.

Yahoo! Resume Services

```
http://www.yahoo.com/Business_and_
Economy/Companies/Employment_Services/
Resume_Services/
```

It lists 80 or more resume sites.

JobHunt Resume Banks

```
http://rescomp.stanford.edu/jobs/
resume.shtml
```

It listed 36 resume sites, last time I visited; it is very up-to-date.

JobSmart Descriptions of Major Resume Banks

```
http://jobsmart.org/internet/
resbanks.htm
```

It lists a *sampler* of free sites (it lists six, in great detail) and for-fee sites (five, in great detail).

Yahoo! jobs newsgroups

```
http://www.yahoo.com/Business_and_
Economy/Employment/Jobs/Usenet/
```

Leaving the Web, there are the Usenet Newsgroups on the Internet where resumes can also be posted. Yahoo! has lists of these, at the above site. You will note that not everything on Yahoo!'s list is devoted to resumes (it calls them "jobs wanted" or "requests for employment" when they are). The remainder on this list are actually job listings by employers (you can detect this when it calls them "jobs offered" or "jobs available").

Remember, if you post your resume on *all* of these sites, and absolutely *nothing* happens, do not take it personally. Reread (five times) my overall evaluation of resume sites, that appeared on pp. 37 ff. In a nutshell: it ain't you; it's the system.

(If you try putting your resume on the Net, and after a time still can't find a job, see page 79 ff.)

3.

Career Counseling

Career Counseling Sites on the Internet

Well, I'm happy to report that there are some very interesting career centers on the Web. Most of them belong to universities and colleges.

I wish I could say the same for the *non-collegiate* commercial career counseling centers on the Web and elsewhere -- but having roamed a number of such places online, myself, for upwards of two years now -- *and* having talked to other *Web-savvy* career counselors around the nation to gather *their* impressions, I must report that we have found the situation downright depressing.

What one would *hope* to find on the commercial sites, are:
- detailed answers to the questions raised by job-hunters, running a couple of paragraphs or on up to a page or so;
- written by *truly competent* career-counselors;
- at no cost to the job-hunter;
- and without the career counselor or counseling center trying to sell additional services and products -- often *expensive* services (*hidden agendas*).

The reality is sometimes far from this. In fact, my various colleagues around the country feel that some of the career advice online is absolutely awful. As I have read some of the "answers" to job-hunters' questions on the Web, my hair has turned gray (but then, I'm 70 years old -- maybe my hair turned gray for other reasons). To be sure, the Web is wonderful. But, the fact that inept job-hunting advice is on the Web in living color doesn't magically make that advice un-inept. *Caveat emptor!*

Having said that, let me add: I think this picture has improved *tremendously* in the last half year or so, and I'm much encouraged by what I see. Some really good people have been coming online lately. Mary-Ellen Mort's site, *JobSmart,* is a case in point.

I think the situation will continue to improve.

How Effective?

My personal estimate of the effectiveness of career counseling sites on the Internet: **10 percent**. That is, out of every 100 people who seek career counseling on the Internet, 10 of them will find a job thereby, due to the coaching that they pick up there. I think 90 will not.

Parachute Picks: Career Counseling Sites

To begin with, there are some *gateway* sites that list career counseling sites on the Internet. The two I like the best are:

Catapult Career Office
```
http://www.jobweb.org/catapult/
homepage.htm
```
It has a list of college career counseling offices that have sites on the Internet, sorted by country (the United Kingdom, the United States, Canada, and Australia) and region -- within the United States, anyway. It's not thorough: I know of many colleges that are on the Web, but are not on this list. Still, it's a good place to begin.

RPI Career Resource
```
http://www.rpi.edu/dept/cdc/
homepage.html
```
This site, maintained by Rensselaer Polytechnic Institute, also has a good list of career counseling sites, at least for the United States.

As for individual sites, you might want to begin, first of all, by going back and looking at some of the famous sites that I mentioned under "Job Listings." Many of them have career counseling as well -- career advice, career articles, lists of helpful books for the job-hunter, and that sort of thing.

Others worth noting:

JobSmart

http://jobsmart.org/

This is a *great,* relatively new career counseling site, and one of my favorites, developed by Mary-Ellen Mort, for California.

Career Paradise

http://www.emory.edu/CAREER/

This site, hosted by the career center at Emory University in Atlanta, was created 1/4/96, with lots of impudent humor -- attributable to John H. Youngblood, who was its Webmaster from then until 8/24/96. Unfortunately, he has moved on and now some of the information, such as that on the "Colossal List of Career Links," is somewhat out of date. Still, what it does have is helpful, and this site has a fine summary of the career planning process.

The Career Action Center

http://www.careeraction.org/

Formerly located in Palo Alto, this Center is one of the most famous career counseling places in the U.S. The Center has recently moved, but its Web site hasn't changed.

Parachute Picks:
Career Counseling Manuals or Books

Now, aside from career counseling centers, the Internet can offer you elementary career counseling or job-hunting manuals. Here are some interesting sites, in that regard:

Creative Job Search

http://mn.jobsearch.org/cjs/
cjs_site/cjs-home.htm

This site, maintained by the Minnesota Department of Economic Security, has put together the equivalent of a job-search manual, on their "Creative Job Search" page. Mark this: these authors really understand what *skills* are (refreshing, on the Internet). Employment applications, interviews, etc. are also covered.

Career Services at the University of Waterloo

http://www.adm.uwaterloo.ca/infocecs/
CRC/manual-home.html

The career center at the University of Waterloo has put together a thorough detailed description to guide you through your job-hunt; its self-assessment manual is one of the best on the Internet.

Job Search Guide: Strategies for Professionals

http://www.cabrillo.cc.ca.us/connect/
docs/jobsearch.html

An amazingly thorough 74-page introduction to the job search is put out by the **United States Employment Service**, at this site; the manual can be printed out on your home printer.

The CareerNET Resource and Development Center

http://www.ldol.state.la.us:80/
career1/ldolcp.htm

If you want a nice list of career books before you go down to the bookstore or library, this site, sponsored by the Louisiana Department of Labor, has such a list, often with extensive outlining and critique of each book.

Parachute Picks: Miscellaneous Career Counseling Helps

Myers-Briggs (personality typing newsgroup archive)
http://sunsite.unc.edu/personality/

The Myers-Briggs *instrument* is all the rage in Career Counseling these days. It is not on the Internet. But there is a personality-type test online ("The Keirsey Temperament Test") which you fill out online, whence it automatically scores itself, and gives you a Myers-Briggs–like code. It is to be found at this newsgroup's list about "personality typing systems" (this does not refer to a computer keyboard).

Myers-Briggs FAQ: A Summary of Personality Typing

http://sunsite.unc.edu/personality/
faq-mbti.html

If you want more of an explanation of Personality Typing, plus a brief summary of the sixteen personality types, go to this site.

The Holland Game

http://www.phlab.missouri.edu/~cppcwww/
holland.html

Readers of *What Color Is Your Parachute?* who like the "Party Exercise" that I invented (based on John Holland's RIASEC system) will find it, sans *diagram,* but with the same wording, at this University of Missouri site.

Informational Interviewing

http://danenet.wicip.org/jets/
jet-9407-p.html

This important technique, serving as an alternative to the traditional job-hunt, is explained and discussed at this site.

4.

Contacts

Sites on the Internet Where You Can Make Contacts

I think this is the next-to-most-helpful use of the Internet in job-hunting because, in its essence, *all job-hunting is a search for people contacts* -- that is, for links between you and an employer, or between you and clients. Contacts are the name of the game (at least in *creative* job-hunting).

Through the Internet, you can contact people all over the globe.

If you know who you want to reach, you can do it instantly, without waiting five days for a letter to get there -- by using e-mail.

If you don't know who (or whom) you want to reach, you can locate people through:

- **gopher sites** ("Gopher" is a menu-driven system of getting information; it pre-dates the Web, but its sites are accessible through your Web browser.)

- **newsgroups** (A "newsgroup" is like a discussion group that meets on an electronic bulletin board -- devoted to some field of interest -- where each of you leaves messages for one another on that bulletin board. These newsgroups are located on a part of the Internet called *Usenet,* and are accessible through your Web browser here *if* your Internet service provider gives you *Usenet access.*)

- **e-mailing lists** (Also called "mailing lists," these are discussion groups like *Usenet,* except that every message from every member on the list is automatically sent to your e-mail address. You don't have to go anywhere to get the messages -- they come to you.)

- **chat rooms** (There are also *"chat-rooms"* on the Internet and on commercial services such as *America Online,* where you "meet with" other people, online, and have a chat with each other in real time -- via your keyboard input.)

In sum, the number of contacts you can make online, is absolutely mind-boggling. Any faraway place that interests you, you'll likely find a contact online. Any question you need an answer to, you'll likely find someone online who knows the answer. Any organization where you need to know how to meet "the-person-who-has-the-power-to-hire," you'll likely find someone on line who knows somebody who . . .

You will want to remember, of course, that anyone you contact on the Internet should be approached -- as in *real* life -- respectfully, politely, courteously, and with keen awareness on your part that this is a very busy person, who may or may not be able to respond. If they do give you any help, e-mail thank-you notes should *always* be sent to them, *promptly* (within three days) for the help they gave you.

How Effective?

My personal estimate of the effectiveness of going online, in getting a job: **20 percent** -- that is, out of every 100 people who make contact with people on the Internet, 20 of them will find a job as a result. I think 80 will not.

Parachute Picks: Sites to Make Contacts

Finding Newsgroups or Mailing Lists

`http://www.synapse.net/~radio/finding.htm`

As I mentioned above, one of your best bets for finding contacts is to discover a newsgroup or e-mailing list, centered around the field of interest in which you are trying to find a contact. This site here, run by Synapse Internet, has a good list of such places, and how to find them.

The Contact Center Network -- Directory

`http://www.contact.org/`

This excellent site lists over 8,000 organizations, publications, nonprofits, and community organizational interests. You can browse around the world, by country, or by keyword. Great site!

Publicly Accessible Mailing Lists

`http://www.neosoft.com/internet/paml/`

Finding contacts by interest field can also be done on this site, maintained by NeoSoft™. It has a wonderful list that can be accessed by subject, name, or title.

555-1212.com

`http://www.555-1212.com/`

Once you know the name of a contact, you of course want to be able to find them. This site links to a number of *directories*, all on one page (it's a *long* page -- be sure to scroll down). You'll find some nifty features, including "a reverse directory." It includes on its page, three directories that I find particularly useful, myself. They are:

Switchboard

`http://www.switchboard.com/`

This site looks for *complete* addresses and phone numbers. In my experience, it finds people that some of the other directories know nothing about. It has saved my life, more than once.

WhoWhere?

`http://www.whowhere.com/`

Well, I can't always find what I want here. But what it does, it does exceedingly well. It searches not only for an individual's address, phone number, and/or e-mail address, but it will even search a phone number to see who it belongs to. (Scary!) It lists *companies* on the Net, and in the Yellow Pages, as well -- in case you're trying to reach someone at a particular company.

Four11

```
http://www.Four11.com/cgi-bin/
Four11Main?fonesearch&FormId=
```

Just type in the name of the person and the state they live in, and this program *may* turn up their address, zipcode, and phone number. However, it *sometimes* omits streets, just when I want them most. And, like all these search directories, it can turn up *dozens* of similar names in large metropolitan areas -- and sometimes the addresses are outdated or wrong.

My overall advice, if you're looking for a specific person by name, as a potential contact: be *sure* to use all three of these programs. Sometimes two of them will miss, but the third will tell you exactly what you want to know.

Use `http://www.555-1212.com/`
if all three of them fail.

5.

Research

Information or Research Sites on the Internet

All job-hunting is a search for information. And the Internet is a superlative place to find information, without the limitations that a normal public library would have. You can access the Internet on holidays, you can access it 24 hours a day, and you don't have to even leave the house.

The amount of information you can find on the Internet today is mind-boggling. But be aware of this before you start: when you're doing job-hunting research on the Internet, you can find so many interesting side-paths, that it can divert you from your job-hunt or career-change for weeks, *all the while giving you the illusion that you are hard at work on it. "Hey, what do you mean I'm not working very hard on my job-hunt? I spent three hours yesterday surfin' the Net."*

It's the sidepaths that can kill you. In the past month, while surveying job-hunting sites, I found the following alluring sidepaths: I suddenly grew curious about the names of the Seven Dwarves. *Found that, easily.* I then wanted to know the words to an old song. *Found that, easily.* Wanted to know what films a certain actor had appeared in, throughout his career. *Found that, easily.* I remembered that a member of my family was going to school in Australia. *Easily found* a map of the campus, a map of the town, and an academic calendar for next year, all of which I could print out *in living color.*

Fascinating. Eating up the hours. But as I said: these sidepaths can kill you -- leaving you no time for your actual job-hunt. If you're going to do any of your job-hunting on the Internet, bring carloads of self-discipline. I mean: carloads.

How Effective?

The effectiveness of online research in getting a job? Well, **that depends** of course on what kind of information you're looking for, how essential it is for your job-hunt or career-change that you find this piece of information, etc., etc. In other words, it's impossible to say. We can, however, say this about job-hunting on the Internet & World Wide Web: it can be a great adjunct to your job-hunt, *if rightly used.*

Parachute Picks: Research Sites: Standard Reference Works

I mean things like: *dictionaries, encyclopedias, access to libraries on the Internet,* and the like.

LDOL CareerNet Reference
http://www.ldol.state.la.us:80/
career1/hp_refer.htm

This site has a good list of reference works, including ERIC, CARL, Usenet Search, an Online Dictionary of Computing, Internet Public Library, a congressional bill-tracking database, directories to nonprofit organizations, etc. Extremely useful.

Yahoo! Reference

http:www.yahoo.com/Reference/

Yahoo! also has a list of reference works, but I found it easier to find *job-hunting-related works* on the Career-Net site, above.

SunSITE LibWeb

http://sunsite.berkeley.edu/Libweb/

This Berkeley Digital Library SunSITE has a good list of libraries that are online, in the U.S. and throughout the world. They, in turn, have many resources on their own individual online sites.

Parachute Picks: Research Sites: Occupational Fields

The Occupational Outlook Handbook

http://stats.bls.gov/ocohome.htm

This is the place to begin, *of course*, in researching particular occupational fields. It is the Bureau of Labor Statistics' official handbook.

Bureau of Labor Statistics' Projections

http://stats.bls.gov/news.release/
ecopro.toc.htm

You may wish to supplement the Outlook Handbook with figures and articles concerning the projected future of particular occupations. In that case, this is the site to visit.

JobTrak College/Major Index

http://www.jobtrak.com/docs/
collegelist.html

If you want a list of possible fields for you to consider, hundreds of them are listed here. If, further, you want to take a course of study or a degree program in any of these fields, this site lists which universities, colleges or two-year colleges offer such majors.

AT&T Toll-Free Internet Directory

http://www.tollfree.att.net/dir800/

If the above list is too narrow for you, and you want more choices, there is another way to generate ideas of fields you might be interested in -- and that is, by going through the Yellow Pages and looking at the Yellow Page *categories.* Such categories are roughly equivalent to "fields." You can find them at this site (choose "Browse by Category" once you're there).

Yahoo! Professional Organizations

http://www.yahoo.com/Economy/
Organizations/Professional/

If you want to explore a particular field (or fields) further, you want to go to their *Associations, or Professional Associations,* and many of them are listed here.

Job Databases by Professional Societies/Other Institutions

http://www.rpi.edu/dept/cdc/society/

You can also find such a list of such Associations or *Professional Societies* on this site.

The Argus Clearinghouse: Business & Employment

http://www.clearinghouse.net/tree/
busemp.html

If you want *articles* related to particular fields, this is the site to visit (it's called "Internet Job Surfer").

JobSmart Salary Info

http://jobsmart.org/tools/salary/
index.htm

For some job hunters, no research of a particular occupation is complete until they've found out what it pays. For them, and for you, the best list of salary surveys on the Net (hands down!) is at this site. It has over 120 of them.

Pencom Career Center

`http://www.pencomsi.com/careerhome.html`

This site also deals with salary research. It offers an interactive salary guide, as well as other 'goodies': nationwide job listings, and articles on particular careers.

Parachute Picks: Research Sites: Companies, Organizations, or Businesses

---

Once you've researched an occupational field, or occupation, you will of course want information on particular companies, organizations, or businesses in your chosen field. To help you in this task, a number of Internet search engines and directories have compiled lists of company directories for you:

Yahoo! Company Directories

`http://www.yahoo.com/Business_and_ Economy/Companies/Directories/`

Here's the beginning of some help. You'll probably need additional directories, though, such as the three which follow.

Accufind Business/Corporate Resource Sites

`http://nln.com/`

This site has a very helpful bunch of directories for you to try.

100hot

`http://www.100hot.com/`

More lists of directories and companies.

Excite's Company Reviews

`http://www.excite.com/`

More lists of directories and companies. Needless to say, these four sites, cited here, have some *overlap*. But each one knows things the others don't.

Mansfield U. Business/Economics Reference

`http://www.mnsfld.edu/~library/`
`mu-biz.html`

Once you know the name of an organization or company, you'll of course want to be able to research it. To get you started, Mansfield University's library online has a wonderful collection of *Business and Economics References* -- Business Yellow Pages, Canadian Statistics, Hoover's, Edgar (SEC database), etc.

Starting Point-Business

`http://www.stpt.com/busine.html`

Starting Point also has a great collection of Commercial Directories at this site.

Business Job Finder

`http://www.cob.ohio-state.edu/dept/`
`fin/osujobs.htm`

For those interested in business careers, or careers in finance, accounting, or management, The Fisher College of Business at Ohio State has this "Business Job Finder" just for you.

LookupUSA

`http://www.abii.com/`

And now, to get really detailed. This site, sponsored by American Business Information, Inc., lists 88 million households and 11 million businesses. They can give you a full company profile with key executives, number of employees, sales volume, lines of business, fax numbers, and more. A profile is available, by phone call, for $3.

IBM InfoMarket

`http://www.infomarket.ibm.com/`

This site has information on more than 10 million companies. But if you want a detailed report, it will cost you.

Dun & Bradstreet

`http://www.dbisna.com/dbis/product/`
`secure.htm`

Well of course *they* have information about companies, more than 10 million of them. But, again, if you want anything detailed, these reports will be for a price.

Big Book

`http://www.bigbook.com`

As far as *locating* a business is concerned, once you know its name, there are *huge* telephone directories on the Web, which are searchable by name. This one will not only give you the address, but also draw you a map showing you where the business is located. Only drawback: the maps are not always accurate, key streets are not named at times *unless you zoom all the way in*, and sometimes the addresses are as much as a year out of date. (Bad news if the place moved in the last 12 months.) Still it's a good start.

BigYellow

http://s13.bigyellow.com/

NYNEX has another such directory, helpful in locating the phone number and address of a particular business, anywhere in the country.

See also the directories listed under contact sites on pp. 58 ff.

Parachute Picks: Research Sites: Special Populations or Special Problems

If you have a special problem or special population in mind, give it to your favorite search engine, and see what it turns up. I have listed a sampler of the *kind* of things to be found on the Internet, in this regard.

Resources for Minorities

VJF Internet Resources for Minorities

http://www.vjf.com/pub/docs/
jobsearch.html

Your search engine will find such things as this site belonging to **Virtual Job Fair**, "The Global Village: Resources for Minorities on the Internet." First rate.

Resources for Women

WWWomen

http://www.wwwomen.com/

Your search engine will find such things as this site which calls itself "The Premier Search Directory for Women Online."

Pleiades Women's Directory

http://www.pleiades-net.com/lists/
orgs.html

Your search engine will find such things as this site belonging to **Pleiades Network**. They call it the "Women's Directory."

FeMiNa

http://www.femina.com/

A number of good resources for women are also listed on this site.

iGuide -- Women's Careers
http://www.iguide.com/insites/13/3/1/
index.htm

Resources for Gay and Lesbian Job-Hunters

Lavender Pages

http://www.lavenderpages.com/

Your search engine will find such things as this site. It is a San Francisco Bay Area resource, listing over 1,200 businesses and organizations for the lesbian, gay and bisexual community -- not just in San Francisco. Very comprehensive.

Bach Personnel

http://www.best.com/~bach/hstory.html

Your search engine will also find personnel agencies "targeted at, but not limited to, the gay and lesbian community." This is a well-known one in San Francisco.

Resources for the Elderly

Social Security Administration

http://www.ssa.gov/pubs/10069.html

Your search engine will find such sites as this one, dealing with Social Security and retirement. Among other things, this site has useful information about benefits, and advice about how and when to retire.

Resources for People with Disabilities

The Job Accommodation Network
`http://janweb.icdi.wvu.edu/kinder/`
Your search engine will find such sites as this one, which gives information particularly related to the Americans with Disabilities Act.

Resources for Those Seeking Work with Nonprofits

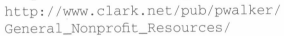

Nonprofit Resources Catalog
`http://www.clark.net/pub/pwalker/`
`General_Nonprofit_Resources/`
Your search engine will find a lot of sites dealing with nonprofits. What is unusual, I think, about these sites, is that they are almost all uniformly excellent. But, in my estimation, this site has the best list, an outstanding one maintained by Phillip A. Walker.

The Contact Directory to Nonprofits
`http://www.contact.org/sample/dir.htm`
This site has some wonderful lists, categorized by field, state, and country (the directory is worldwide).

Magellan

http://www.mckinley.com/

This site also has an excellent list.

Good Works

http://www.tripod.com/work/goodworks/
search.html

This site, maintained by Tripod, Inc., and aimed at young adults moving from college into the workplace, has a list of nonprofits doing good in the community.

Ralph Nader — Essential Information

http://www.essential.org/goodworks/

Created by Ralph Nader's organization, this site, called "Essential Information," likewise has a section called Good Works, which provides access to the book by that title, and lists some actual job listings.

4Work

http://www.4work.com/

Here you will find job listings from various business and not-for-profit organizations, internships, youth positions, and volunteer work. This site has what looks at first sight like a nifty search tool: by registering your name, e-mail address, keywords, and geographic specifications, you are automatically updated via e-mail whenever a new job listing occurs, that matches your specifications of what you are looking for. That's the good news. The bad news is that their listings seem limited, *to say the least.* The first time I visited this site, it had a *heavy* emphasis on opportunities in Colorado. The second time I visited this site, things looked a little *broader.* Let's hope that trend continues.

Resources for Those Seeking Self-Employment

Working Solo

http://www.workingsolo.com/

Your search engine will find such sites as this one, a "site for independent entrepreneurs," that lists 1,200 business resources for those seeking self-employment. Great site!

Small Business Administration

http://www.sbaonline.sba.gov/

Let us not forget the obvious friend of self-employed businesspersons, the U.S. Small Business Administration, which has *a very helpful* site here, loaded with information.

Yahoo! Small Business Information

http://www.yahoo.com/

Here you can find all kinds of information of interest to the small businessperson, such as stuff about intellectual property (copyrights, etc.) or anything else that you're curious about.

Business Resource Center

http://www.greatinfo.com/business_
cntr/bus_res.html

All kinds of resources for the self-employed can be found at The Information Center's site. It leads you to MoneyHunter, a site for seeking investment for your enterprise -- and other interesting places.

Excite Business Reviews

http://www.excite.com/Reviews/Business/

This search engine has another list of helpful resources for the self-employed.

Resources for Those Interested in Volunteering or in Internships

4Work

http://www.4work.com/

Your search engine will find such sites as this one. I mentioned it earlier. It is of interest here because it has some helpful resources dealing with volunteering and internships.

Resources for Those Seeking Temp Work

Temp Access

`http://www.tempaccess.com/agenlist.html`

Your search engine will find such sites as this one. They have here a particularly good listing of all the temporary agencies in the U.S. that are online. Very useful!

Incidentally, people are always asking me, *what is your vision for the Web: what do you think it should do for job-hunters?* Well, since we're talking about temporary agencies here, I am reminded of the fact that New York City has a truly exemplary use of what the Web could be. It's called **The Red Guide**, and it's found at:

`http://www.panix.com/~grvsmth/redguide/`

In addition to a useful "Tips for Temps" section, it is most importantly a site where people who have worked for temporary agencies in NYC can write in afterwards, about their experience with those agencies. (Choose "Review Database.')

If the Web were to have such sites nationwide, divided by geographical region, and not only for temporary agencies, but all other job-counseling centers, counselors, and services, where job-hunters could report their experiences, positive and negative, then the Web would begin to do something that only it can do, *job-hunt-wise.*

If it were to follow this up by having one unified site in all the world for resumes, one unified site in all the world for job-postings, with powerful search capabilities,

And if it were to follow this up by designing a set of protocols, procedures, and standards -- such as Tim Berners-Lee has designed, and is designing, for the World Wide Web -- as to how job-hunters and employers alike list what they are looking for and what they have to offer, thus enabling job-hunter and employer to at least speak a common language to each other,

Then I think we sould see the Internet begin to fulfill its potential to add something terrific to the job-hunt process, rather than its present tendency to merely ape or *tidy up* the Neanderthal job-hunting system that already existed, out there, long before the Internet ever came along.

Conclusion: If You Don't Find a Job

Well, that is the end of our guide to job-hunting on the Internet. If all of this pays off for you, and you get the job you most desire, *great!* But, if it doesn't, please don't take it personally. Remember the words of Margaret Riley, everybody's favorite expert on electronic job-hunting: "The Internet is merely an added dimension to the traditional job search, and it is not necessarily an easy dimension to add." And let me add: It *doesn't* pay off for huge numbers of people.

Let me show you what I mean:

Reports from the Field:
The Experience of Actual Job-Hunters
Concerning Their Resumes (and Job Listings)
On the Internet This Year

Jobhunter #1. *I have not had any positive reaction to any of my listings of my resume online. The one exception was a headhunter who asked for my resume. You will get a lot of offers from strange companies or people looking for things that I would describe as pyramid schemes.*

Jobhunter #2. *It was a waste of my time . . . not a single reply!*

Jobhunter #3. *I haven't gotten any responses online. My impression is that if you're not in the computer field, you can pretty much forget finding work online.*

Jobhunter #4. *I found the Internet to be very limited, even*

The Internet

for computer employment (which is what I do). Even the "Entry-Level" newsgroup is full of jobs requiring previous experience. Most of the employer listings seem to be looking for another Albert Einstein with just as many years of experience.

Jobhunter #5. *I didn't actually get my job from the Net, though I made a pass at it. But in the end, I probably reverted to old habits rather than pursuing the job search on the Net the way I said I would. At the same time, the Net definitely played a part in my job hunt, as I pursued many of my contacts via e-mail -- much better than making "cold" telephone calls, once I'd gotten an e-mail address for a contact in a company (for some reason, a much easier thing than getting direct phone numbers). If I had it to do over again, I would probably do more to take advantage of the Net . . .*

Jobhunter #6. *I found seeking work online was worthwhile, but I'm in computer programming. After watching the listings for a few weeks, I saw a posting in mid-December which I answered with an e-mailed cover letter and resume. I heard back within a few hours, indicating they would be in touch when they scheduled interviews. While waiting to hear back, I saw another posting for which I considered myself qualified (Note: only two listings that fitted me at all, in four weeks). I answered this one, but never heard back. However, the first one did call me back four weeks later, to set up an appointment, and they offered me the job two weeks after that. I started three weeks after that. But notice how long this process took. While you connect quickly on the Internet, the employment process still moves at a snail's pace "out there." You'll need patience. Big time patience.*

Jobhunter #7. *I feel that online job lists should be viewed with the same healthy skepticism that we offer to want ads. That is, there are many scams, there are comparatively few jobs outside high tech, the government, and academe, and the qualifications sought are either high or highly specialized. Thus, one should not spend any greater time online than he or she would spend looking at the want ads. There is more hype than substance for the so-called average job seeker.*

If you're job-hunting on the Internet, and nothing turns up for you, that's because the Internet (currently) just presents us with the old job-hunting system in a new dress. That system didn't work very well before the Internet, and it doesn't work very well now. But, of course, you want to try it anyway.

My advice is: budget only a certain amount of your total job-hunting time to *the Internet part of your job-search* (I'd say 15% of your time, *max*). Keep tabs on yourself, and if after two weeks you discover that the Internet is *all* you are doing with your life, disconnect, give your modem to a friend, and go back to job-hunting *the old way:* the way people job-hunted before the computer was discovered.

But follow *the creative method of job-hunting,* puh-leaze. The rules are simple: *Know your best and most enjoyable transferable skills. Know what kind of work you want to do, what field you would most enjoy working in. Talk to people who are doing the work you want to do, in that field. Find out how they like the work, how they found their job. Do some research, then, in your chosen geographical area on those organizations which interest you, to find what they do and what kinds of problems/challenges they or their industry are wrestling with. Then identify and seek out the person who actually has the power to hire you at each organization, for the job you want; use your personal contacts -- everyone you know -- to get in to see him or her. Show this person with the power to hire you how you can help them with their problems/needs/challenges; and how you would stand out as "one employee in a hundred." Don't take turndown or rejection personally. Remember, there are two kinds of employers out there: those who will be bothered by your handicaps -- age, background, inexperience, or whatever they are -- and those who won't be, and will hire you, so long as you can do the job. If you get rejected by the first kind of employer, keep persevering, until you find the second.*

In all of this, cut no corners, take no shortcuts.

If you need further help with the job-hunt in general, rather than just with the Internet, go read *The 1997 What Color Is Your Parachute?* It's in all the bookstores. A new, updated edition comes out each year, reaching the bookstores (usually) between November 1st and November 20th.

About: What Color Is Your Parachute?

What Color Is Your Parachute? A Practical Manual for Job-Hunters and Career Changers was first published December 1, 1970. It was self-published, and two thousand copies sold within the first year. A commercial publisher, Ten Speed Press, of Berkeley, California, then asked to publish it, and their first commercially-published edition came out in November, 1972. Its whimsical title was a playful response to the phrase commonly used by career-changers in the '70s: "I've decided I'm gonna bail out." The book, in its subsequent history, has given birth to many expressions in our culture, such as "informational interviewing," "transferable skills," and -- a term the author cordially dislikes -- "golden parachutes."

Parachute has been revised and updated annually since 1975; as well, twice in its history the book has been almost completely rewritten, from scratch (this was the case with the current -- 1997 -- edition, and also in 1992).

Twenty-four thousand people buy the book each month, and there are 5,600,000 copies in print. It is often called "the job hunter's bible." Recent reviews have called it "the Cadillac of job-search books," "the most complete career guide around," "the enduring job-hunter's bible," and "the gold standard of career guides." As the book is rarely advertised, it sells because one person tells another person about it. That's why the Library of Congress' Center for the Book on its 1995-1996 list, listed it as one of "25 Books That Have Shaped Readers' Lives" (alongside such works as Maya Angelou's *I Know Why the Caged Bird Sings,* Saint Exupery's *The Little Prince,* Henry Thoreau's *Walden,* Cervantes' *Don Quixote,* Tolstoy's *War and Peace,* and Mark Twain's *The Adventures of Huckleberry Finn*).

With hundreds of other job-hunting books out there, *Parachute* has kept its title as "the best-selling job-hunting book in the world" for three decades, for seven reasons:

1. It works. It gives a step-by-step process for getting around all the obstacles normally encountered in the job-hunt. Millions of people have *successfully* changed jobs or careers, using its advice.

2. It has a simple structure for doing your job hunt or career change, a *"What, Where, How Method"* that everyone can understand:

- **What** are the transferable skills you most enjoy using?

- **Where** do you want to use those skills? In what favorite fields of knowledge?

- **How** do you find such jobs, that use your favorite skills and favorite fields of knowledge?

3. It is humorous. The author is naturally playful, and his descriptions are often very humorous. Also, the book is filled with cartoons and other stuff designed to make the job hunt a little less solemn and stuffy.

4. The book is visually interesting to work through. It is filled with old lithographs (some of which you will see in the body of this book), tables, charts, and cartoons. It is not just text, text, text.

5. It takes seriously the fact that people are in a great hurry (and has three chapters in the 1997 edition called "For the Impatient Job-Hunter"); but it also takes seriously those who wish to be more thorough (three chapters called "For the Determined Job-Hunter or Career-Changer," as well as "The Quick Job-Hunting Map" -- a series of practical exercises for knowing yourself better).

6. It covers many subjects other job-hunting books don't. The supplemental text in the 1997 edition, called *The Parachute Workbook & Resource Guide*, covers such topics as "dealing with depression while job-hunting," "how to choose a career counselor," with names of counselors all over the country and the world, and "how to find your mission in life," for people of faith.

7. It is always up to date. Its annual revisions allow it to keep up with the latest job-hunting techniques, and the latest changes in the job-market.

Almost any bookstore has the latest edition. If they're sold out, or do not carry it, you can order the book (on the Web) at www.amazon.com or by phone directly from the publisher, Ten Speed Press, in Berkeley, California, at 1-800-841-BOOK (*that's* 2665).

A Beginner's Primer:

What Exactly
Is the Internet?

What Exactly Is the Internet?

We may think of the last three decades, *computer-wise*, in broad brush strokes such as these . . .

The '70s may be thought of as largely The Era of the **Mainframe** Computer. It was a huge thing that could fill a whole room. Hooked up to it were *terminals*, smaller machines that were used to run programs on the mainframe. (The mainframe acted as what would later be called a *server*-- defined as anything that provides services to another computer.)

With the coming of the '80s we moved into a new era: The Era Of The **Desktop** Computer. Manufacturers were able to put on each person's desk a computer that was self-contained with its own data-storage system-- ultimately, hard disk(s). These were computers requiring connection to nothing else, and, by the late '80s, nearly the equal of some of the old mainframes, in terms of computing power and speed.

With the coming of the '90s we moved into still another era, which may be thought of, loosely, as The **Union** of Mainframe and Desktop. A *kind-of mainframe* has returned, not as a replacement for the desktop computer, but as an adjunct to it. What is different from the '70s is that this *kind-of mainframe* is not constructed as one big computer filling a huge room, but as a number of networks of computer sites around the world deciding to voluntarily link up with each other - - desktop and mainframe alike - - so that *together* they act *as if* they were a *kind-of humongous mainframe*.

And the name of this *mainframe-like thing* is <u>The</u> Internet, 'cause it's a series of links *between* (hence: *Inter-*) a whole *network of networks* (hence: *-Net*) of computers around the world.

When, therefore, you connect to the Internet today you are seeking out this thing we might call (by the way of *very, very* loose metaphor) *The World's Largest Mainframe*, and linking it with your desktop computer - - whereupon you too become *part of the Internet* - - which has one part in Michigan, one part in Sweden, one part in Worcester, one part in Australia, one part in Berkeley, and so on and so forth.

But in spite of the scatteredness of its parts, what is ingenious about the thing is that it performs essentially as though it were one.

The Birth of "The Blues"

I characterized the Internet, above, as a creature of the '90s. Actually, it existed for a couple of decades before that. It just never became really popular with *the masses* until the '90s. It is easy to explain why.

First proposed in the '60s by RAND Corporation, MIT, and UCLA, the Internet actually began in 1969 as part of the Pentagon's Advanced Research Projects. Their concern was to ensure that information could be sent around the world in peacetime or wartime, even if particular cities - - hence computer sites - - were destroyed (*this is why the Internet breaks down a message into electronic "packets," then has those packets take* random *routes to their destination, where they are then reassembled*).

The Pentagon's concerns aside, the Internet quickly got adopted as a kind of high-speed electronic post office, and in the 1980s expanded to include the National Science Foundation's supercomputer sites, as well as university, library, and research centers' sites.

Nonetheless, it remained largely the domain of a kind of "computer aristocracy": defense people, computer programmers, and academic types. It didn't attract a wider audience for a number of reasons. For one thing, there were several different *models of data*, hence *protocols* or *rules*, that each Internet *host* could adopt. These protocols had such names as *telnet, ftp, gopher, usenet, listserv, e-mail,* and the like, and each node or host computer on the Internet could decide what model or protocol it wished to adopt for its site.

What these protocols had in common was that their data appeared on your computer screen as essentially *text, text, text* - - no color, no pictures, no pizzazz, no nothin'. (*You* could *download pictures to your own computer, but they were binary files which*

had been encoded, *and basically looked like a mess of gibberish - - until, once they were downloaded to your desktop computer, you* de-coded *them, back into their original binary code. Then, and only then, a picture would slowly appear on your desktop. It all was and is a very big royal pain.*)

And that was the state of the Internet when, finally, along came the *World Wide Web.* At last: Lights! Camera! Action! Text in colors: yellows, reds, and blues!

The World Wide Web

In 1990, Tim Berners-Lee, at CERN, the European Particle Physics Laboratory in Geneva, Switzerland, conceived the idea of applying an already existent technology called *hypertext* to networked computers. Thus was born (a year later) a new Internet protocol, destined to be called *the World Wide Web.*

Hypertext was used by Tim to magically transport you to a different computer site, different file, etc., *among networked computers* anywhere on the Internet, anywhere in the world - - when you mouse-clicked on a designated word, series of words, graphic, or other *hyperlinks* on your screen.

This enabled users of the Web to leap from one Internet site to another, like a gazelle. In fact, at a time of day when the Web isn't overloaded with traffic, this leaping can be as fast as one to five seconds, from site to site. (*On slow days, of course, it can take much longer, and sometimes a site won't even come up on your computer, because too many people are trying to con-tact it at the same time - -and it is overloaded.*)

In a sense, this wasn't new; the protocol called *gopher* al-ready enabled you to leap around this quickly in *gopherspace* on the Internet. But on the Web, married to this ability *to leap* was the ability *to display pictures, graphics, charts, visuals, and sound,* on your computer monitor. Even the old *text, text, text* could be all gussied up, in colors, so that it looked *pretty.*

In terms of the *state of the art* of the Internet, this was like going from radio to color television, in the blink of an eye.

You, the idle consumer, could now get on the Internet, and instead of looking at *text, text, text,* you could see some really interesting graphics and color and visuals on your desktop computer screen. With the World Wide Web, the Internet had acquired a new face, *inter-face,* that is, and new makeup. It had color. It had pictures. It looked *wonderful.*

Moreover, you could create your own "*Web site*" and "*Web page,*" if you wished, and on that page (*or pages*) display whatever you wanted to. It was, and is, democracy in action.

With the invention of *the Web* interface, the Internet suddenly became *really* interesting to average, everyday people. People perked up. The Internet started attracting the masses, by the millions. Even if you didn't have access to a computer at work, a desktop computer at home could give you access to the Internet with just a *modem* (installed or added to your computer), a *telephone line* running from the phone company's wall plug to your modem, and some *Internet Service Provider* - - in some cases your phone company, who, for a fee, would connect you to the Internet.

Then why is it that 84% of U.S. households, currently, aren't yet connected? Well, for a variety of reasons. Cost is one. The learning curve that is required (it is often *steep*) is another. I would say that your feelings about the Internet will largely depend on how many experiences you have that are described in the left-hand column on the next page, vs. how many experiences you have that are described in the right-hand column.

HAPPY EXPERIENCES	UNHAPPY EXPERIENCES
The computer equipment necessary for going online is at hand, or easy for you to acquire.	The computer equipment necessary for going online is not at hand, and would be expensive for you to acquire.
The modem is already installed inside your computer, or else connecting it to the computer is "a piece of cake."	Connecting the modem to the computer is a process so difficult it can drive you to tears of frustration.
Getting an online provider who has a local access phone number is easy.	Finding a decent online provider where you live, who has a local access phone number, is extremely difficult.
Hooking up via the online provider is easy, because they give you all the information you need in order to be able to do it easily, and they stand by with telephone troubleshooting. Additionally, you have friends who have the same kind of computer you do, are already on the Internet, and are anxious to guide and help you all the way.	Hooking up via the online provider is difficult, because they give you none or little of the information you need in order to be able to do it correctly, and their technicians are unavailable or ignorant of your system. To compound the difficulties, you have no friends who are already on the Internet. Hence, you are basically working blind, here, and are ready to cry at how difficult this all is.
The online provider is inexpensive.	Charges mount by the minute, while you are online to the Web.
You can usually dial right into the Web, without any trouble, through your online provider.	You get the equivalent of constant busy signals from your online provider many times when you try to get on the Internet; their equipment is often overloaded or "down." (AOL comes to mind.)

You have a modem which runs somewhere between 28.8K bps and 128K bps, hence images and Web pages load rather quickly.	You have a modem which runs at 14.4K bps or less, hence images and Web pages load painfully slowly.
Once you are on the Web, you zoom. Your favorite search engine appears on the screen almost immediately, you choose a site and ask your browser to take you there, and you are there almost immediately.	No matter what the speed of your modem, "connections are maddeningly slow, and systems often impenetrable." (*Neil Winton, Reuter.*) E.g., once you are connected to the Web, your favorite search engine does not appear on the screen. Period. *You can't go anyplace.* Or, your browser does appear, you choose a site, and ask your browser to take you there, but you run into a logjam. Or you are rejected with some such message as: "The server may not be accepting connections or may be busy. Try again later." You're going to have to come back later (try midnight) before you can get in.
You can always find the Web page that you are seeking.	You can't find a Web page that you know is out there. You get a message like: "404 Not Found.," or "This server has no DNS." But you *know* it's out there, somewhere.
The Web page you want to see comes up your screen almost immediately.	It takes too long to download and view the Web pages you want.
When you reach a particular site, you discover it was exactly as advertised, and you find just what you want.	When you reach a particular site, you discover *they lied.* E.g., they claim 15,000 employers are listing their vacancies on that site, but at the time you call you find only 22. Or they claim they have *nationwide job listings,* but you discover *that* totals only 50 -- one for each state. And so forth. And so on.

In sum, I agree with the words of Margaret Riley, everybody's favorite expert on electronic job-hunting: "The Internet is merely an added dimension to the traditional job search, and it is not necessarily an easy dimension to add."

But if you're determined to try it, my advice is: budget only a certain amount of your total job-hunting time to *the Internet part of your job search* (I'd say 15% of your time, *max*).

If you're experienced on the Internet, dive in; if you're new to the Internet, I'd think more seriously about whether or not this is the time to plunge in, when you've got so many other things you should be doing right now (like, inventorying your skills, doing *The Quick Job-Hunting Map*, etc.).

For beginners, here is a brief overview of how you start *surfin' the Web*. Once you are connected to the Internet, your computer monitor will require some kind of *Web* browser, such as Netscape Navigator™, which I use here as my illustration.

Once you have that program, some kind of Web browser, you start it up, and eventually "a page" will be displayed on your computer that looks *more or less* like the one on page 98. (*The look of this Netscape Navigator™ "page" may have changed dramatically by the time this falls into your hands.*)

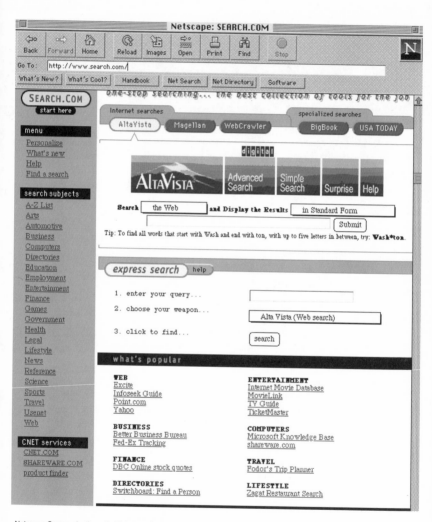

Once you have brought up a search "page" like this, you will wonder what you are staring at. Well, you are staring at a *search engine*, and its regular form - - waiting to be filled in, but not yet filled in.

To conduct a search, you type within the white box by: **1. Search for . . .** some keyword or words indicating your query or interest, and then you mouse-click on the *Search* button next to: **4. Begin search . . .**

What kind of keywords do you type? Well, you might type in words such as "jobs AND Seattle," if that were your interest. Or "career advice," or "companies," "Microsoft," "weather," "social careers," or whatever. Anything about which you're looking for more information.

The engine will then search with lightning speed (we hope) through its entire index of the Internet (*the very bottom of your browser's screen tells you what it's doing*) after which it will give you a list, on screen, of whatever it's found that even *vaguely* matches what you asked for.

If you see something you like, on that list - - *you may not* - - you mouse-click on the file name, and magically *the Web* transports you to the site on the Internet that has that file, no matter where in the world it may be physically located. Voilà! The file opens up, and your browser displays it on your computer. *Unless, of course, you've run into a traffic jam on the information superhighway - - in which case, you'll have to come back, a few hours from now.*

IF YOU KNOW THE URL OF A SITE

You won't need to do a search if you already know **the electronic address** of the site you want to visit, sometimes called its "**Location**" or "**URL**" -- *which stands for Uniform Resource Locator.* For example you may know (*from memory, from a friend, from a newspaper article, or whatever*) that the URL for the search engine/directory called *Yahoo* is:

`http://www.yahoo.com/`

In which case, you go to the box called "Location" that is on the second level down, of your browser, and delete whatever is in there. Then you type all of this new electronic address (*carefully*) into that box, hit the return key on your computer, and -- magically -- your browser will take you to *Yahoo,* wherever it is in the world.

Because the URL leads directly to the site and file, this is the reason every company or venture is putting their URL at the bottom of their newspaper or magazine ad -- that is, assuming they have a page on the Web.

URLs are *tres* important. But even if you were to learn the URLs of, say, all the famous employment sites on the Internet, such as America's Job Bank, the Career Center, Career Mosaic, E-Span, the Monster Board, On-Line Career Center, etc., you could not possibly keep up with what's on the Internet in general, and the World Wide Web in particular.

I quoted earlier the words of Mary-Ellen Mort, founder of the wonderful site *JobSmart,* who said that cataloging the Web is essentially like trying to catalog an active mudslide.

Organizations, groups, and individuals are coming on board the Web at a hair-raising rate: a new *Web site* with its distinctive *Web page* (or pages) gets added every ten minutes, or less. Consequently, as I write, there are at least 30 million Web pages found on 225,000 computers around the world, plus three million articles from 14,000 Usenet news groups. Pages are moving, sites are dying, new sites are being born *endlessly*. And, as Mary-Ellen also points out, URLs *go bad* faster than an egg salad; which means they get replaced, or become outdated.

A BEGINNER'S PRIMER
CONCERNING SEARCH DEVICES

In other words, we're dead on the Internet unless we have a table of contents or an index. Fortunately for you and for me, people have come up with an index to the Internet - - actually a number of *indices*. As an overall category these are loosely all called *Search Engines*. They have weird names, like: *Yahoo, Lycos, Alta Vista, Excite, WebCrawler, Infoseek, NlightN, Hot-Bot, Open Text,* and *Magellan*. But, weird names aside, once you are on the Internet, you are going to become very familiar with some or all of these, because without them, you'll *never* solve the Internet. Said someone in last year's newspaper, "The Internet is a treasure-trove of information, but finding data is next to impossible without software to scout through the network."[1]

Amen, brother. And again I say, Amen.

Hence, the things that are most critical for you to understand, and be at home with on the Web, are not the URLs of famous sites, but the search engines. It's the only way you are going to keep up with what's on the Internet in general, and the World Wide Web in particular.

---

1. George Avalos, staff writer for the *Contra Costa Times,* 5/31/96.

Before we get to them, let's rehearse a few important truths.

To begin with, all search engines are not created equal. Each one indexes the Internet in its own unique way.

For example, some of these search engines, such as *Alta Vista* and *Lycos*, attempt to cover **the whole Web**.

Some of these, such as *Yahoo* and *WebCrawler* or *Infoseek*, try to cover only **the most popular sites** - - hence they are technically called *directories*, rather than *search engines*.

Some of these attempt to cover a multitude of search engines or directories - - technically called *search services*, such as *MetaCrawler* or *Savvy Search*.

And some of these search engines, directories, or services - - such as the *Point* and *C/Net* - - attempt **to evaluate sites**, as to usefulness, content, and attractiveness.

And some of these have formed alliances - - *Yahoo* with *Alta Vista*, *Excite* with *Magellan*, etc. - - which are producing hybrids, difficult to label.

Anyway, *currently*, Netscape Navigator™ has a good detailed description of each current search engine, directory, or search service, at:

`http://home.netscape.com/home/`
`internet-search.html`

But we are not through. Further complicating matters, there are search devices which attempt to explore *other things* on the Internet. For example, you can search directories of such things as phone numbers, businesses, etc.

And then, there are other types of Internet sites in addition to the Web, such as *Usenet* (newsgroups) sites, *gopher* sites, *ftp* sites, *e-mail* sites, *Listserv,* and the like, which have their own search engine *types*. Gopher sites are searched with two devices called "Archie" and "Veronica."

If you want to know more about these sites and protocols and devices, I refer you to the "Internet Tools Summary" at:

```
http://www.december.com/net/tools/
toc3.html
```

Or you may go to the directory called *Yahoo.* Choose "Computers & the Internet," then choose, "Internet," then choose from that menu whatever you are curious about: *gopher, ftp, Usenet, mailing lists (listservs), electronic mail (e-mail), Archie, Veronica,* or whatever. Currently that menu is at:

```
http://www.yahoo.com/Computers_and
_Internet/Internet/
```

To give you a generalized overview of search devices, I prepared the chart, on the next page, *accurate only as of June 1, 1996.* You will want to use this chart only to get a *sense* of how the different search devices work: the actual description of them will inevitably be *outdated* by the time you get to see this.

Search Engines

	Yahoo	MetaCrawler	c/net Search	Alta Vista	Lycos	Excite
URL Address (no spaces any-where in the address, when you type it in to "Location:")	http://www.yahoo.com/	http://metacrawler.cs.washington.edu:8080/	http://www.search.com/	http://altavista.digital.com/	http://www.lycos.com/	http://www.excite.com/
Type of Search Device	*Directory*	*Search Service:* An almost simultaneous search with many engines*	*Search Service:* Successive searches with several engines**	*Search Engine*	*Search Engine*	*Search Service,* though it calls itself a search engine
Web Pages Catalogued (as of 6/3/96)	Mostly those that are user-submitted	It uses all the pages of all the engines it works with.	The pages catalogued by whatever engine it is using at the time.	30 million Web pages	19 million Web pages	11.5 million Web pages
Can I Browse by Subject?	Yes, this is its great strength: it is *beautifully* organized, by librarians.	No	Yes, and lists *all* search engines for a subject, e.g., *employment* has 13 search engines displayed	No	Yes, using its Service called a2z (A2Z)	Yes, using its Net Directory
What Kinds of Sites Are Included?	The Web	The Web	The Web	The Web Usenet (Newsgroups)	The Web	The Web Usenet (Newsgroups) Reviews Classifieds (from Usenet)

Does It Rate the Sites in Terms of Estimated Relevancy?	No	No. But it sifts thru the listings, eliminating duplicates.	Depends on which engine it's using.	Yes. In this respect, c/net rated it *the* best search engine	Yes, using its Service called Point: http://www.pointcom.com	It tries to. I find it's often wide of the mark.
Strong Suit of This Particular Device	Superb with subjects and popular sites	Searches many engines at the same time	Vast number of search devices (250) altogether	Has highest number of relevant hits on a search; excels at finding obscure info	Has second highest number of relevant hits	Goes far beyond *the Web* in its searches; and stays current
The Downside to This Device	There's a lot on the Web it knows nothing about; but what it does know, is organized beautifully. I love it.	In spite of the fact you can set a time limit for the search, it can sometimes take *forever*.	Nothing that I've discovered (yet).	It *sometimes* lists many irrelevant sites first (in spite of its claims to the contrary), *and* it is often very slow to add new sites.	For a search engine that covers most of the Web, I have found (*during a keyword search*) that it misses many sites that I know are there.	Many have reported being frustrated by its search results (me included).
Similar Search Services	WebCrawler: http://web crawler.com/ also searches mainstream information and by subject as well	SavvySearch: http://guaral di.cs.colostate. edu:2000/does a genuinely simultaneous search, *and* with an even larger number of engines	Galaxy: http://galaxy. tradewave.com/ galaxy.html also has an excellent subject index, by fields	InfoSeek Guide: http://guide. infoseek.com also has Usenet *and you can* browse by subject. Third best engine at finding relevant sites.		

*Yahoo, Alta Vista, Lycos, Excite, InfoSeek Guide, WebCrawler, Open Text, Galaxy, and Inktomi.

**Yahoo, Alta Vista, Lycos, Excite, InfoSeek Guide, Magellan, shareware com (software), and Lifestyle (Time Warner publications).

You will want to keep in mind that the above comparison is bound to change, before the ink is barely dry; some of the latest developments can be found at:

```
http://maxonline.com/webmasters/
whatsnew.htm
```

If you want to know about even more search tools available to you on the Internet, than are mentioned above, a superb list is to be found at:

```
http://www.iglou.com/qis/websearch.html
```

Now that you know how to connect to the Internet, and use search engines, you may want to return to page 7.

For Further Reading

If you feel you could use more help than this book has given you, go to your local bookstore and get one or two books on the following booklist:

The Guide to Internet Job Searching by Margaret F. Riley, Frances Roehm, and Steve Oserman (foreword by Tom Jackson),VGM Career Horizons, a division of NTC Publishing Group, Lincolnwood, Illinois, 1996. *An extraordinary work. If you can buy or read only one book, I suggest that this be it. The authors plan to update it, regularly.*

As I mentioned earlier, this Riley Guide, as it is called, can also be found online at the URL of:

`http://www.jobtrak.com/jobguide/`

Be Your Own Headhunter Online, by Pam Dixon & Sylvia Tiersten. Random House, 1995.

Using the Internet in Your Job Search, by Fred E. Jandt & Mary B. Nemnich. JIST Works, Inc., 1995.

Finding a Job on the Internet, by Alfred Glossbrenner. McGraw-Hill, 1996.

The On-Line Job Search Companion, by James C. Gonyea (foreword by Tom Jackson). McGraw-Hill, 1994.

Hook Up, Get Hired! The Internet Job Search Revolution, by Joyce Lain Kennedy. John Wiley & Sons, Inc., 1995. *Joyce, a famous syndicated columnist who was very kind to me in the early days of* Parachute*, has become a pioneer and an acknowledged leader on the subject of electronic job-hunting, by virtue of this book and two earlier ones on the same subject, namely:*

The Electronic Job Search Revolution, by Joyce Lain Kennedy and Thomas J. Morrow. John Wiley & Sons, Inc., 1995.

Electronic Resume Revolution, by Joyce Lain Kennedy and Thomas J. Morrow. John Wiley & Sons, Inc., 1995.

Electronic Resumes for the New Job Market, by Peter D. Weddle. Impact Publications, 1995.

Guerrilla Marketing On-Line, by Jay Conrad Levinson and Charles Rubin, Houghton Mifflin Co., 1995.

About the Author

Richard Bolles, known the world over as the author of *What Color Is Your Parachute?*, is acknowledged as "America's top career expert" *(Modern Maturity* Magazine*)*, "the one responsible for the renaissance of the career counseling profession in the U.S. over the past decade" *(Money* Magazine*)*, and "the most widely read and influential leader in the whole career planning field" *(U.S. Law Placement Assn.)*. He is listed in *Who's Who In America*, and *Who's Who In the World*. He has been featured in countless magazines (including *Reader's Digest, Fortune, Money Magazine,* and *Business Week)*, newspapers, radio, and TV (CNN, Ted Koppel, on ABC's *Nightline*, Diane Sawyer, on *CBS News*, and many others).

Mr. Bolles was born in Milwaukee, Wisconsin on March 19, 1927. He grew up in Teaneck, New Jersey, and graduated from high school there, in 1945. He served in the U.S. Navy, and worked on Wall Street before attending college. The author's academic background is in engineering, physics, and Biblical studies; he is an alumnus of three institutions of higher education: the *Massachusetts Institute of Technology*, where he majored (but did not graduate) in chemical engineering, *Harvard University*, from which he holds a Bachelor's degree in physics *(cum laude)*, and the *General (Episcopal) Theological Seminary* in New York City, from which he holds a Master's degree in New Testament studies. He is, additionally, a member of Mensa and the recipient of two honorary doctorates.

He lives in the San Francisco Bay Area, is married to Carol Christen, a well-known career counselor in her own right, and has five grown children: Stephen, Mark, Gary, Sharon, and Serena (his stepdaughter). Dick's grandfather was a U.S. congressman, his father an editor for the Associated Press, and his brother the famous investigative reporter, Don Bolles, who was assassinated in Phoenix, Arizona, in 1976. His only other immediate family, a sister, Ann Johnson, lives in Florence, New Jersey.